T0106961

Psychosis in the Produce Department

OTHER BOOKS BY LAUREL ANN BOGEN

Poetry:

Washing a Language
Fission
The Last Girl in the Land of the Butterflies
The Burning: New and Selected Poems, 1970–1990
Rag Tag We Kiss
Do Iguanas Dance, Under the Moonlight?

Fiction:

The Projects
The Great Orange Leonard Scandal

Limited Editions:

Washing a Language
Origami: The Unfolding Heart
The Night Grows Teeth and Other Observations
The Disappearing Act

PSYCHOSIS *in the* Produce Department

New and Selected Poems
1975–2015

LAUREL ANN BOGEN

RED HEN PRESS | *PASADENA, CA*

Psychosis in the Produce Department
Copyright © 2016 by Laurel Ann Bogen
All Rights Reserved

No part of this book may be used or reproduced in any manner whatsoever without the
prior written permission of both the publisher and the copyright owner.

Book layout by Abbey Hastings & Natasha Narkiewicz

Library of Congress Cataloging-in-Publication Data

Names: Bogen, Laurel Ann, author.
Title: Psychosis in the produce department : new and selected poems,
   1975–2015 / Laurel Bogen.
Description: First edition. | Pasadena, CA : Red Hen Press, [2016]
Identifiers: LCCN 2015046620 | ISBN 9781597099936 (softcover)
Subjects: | BISAC: POETRY / General.
Classification: LCC PS3552.O4339 A6 2016 | DDC 811/.54—dc23
LC record available at http://lccn.loc.gov/2015046620

The National Endowment for the Arts, the Los Angeles County Arts Commission, the Los
Angeles Department of Cultural Affairs, the Dwight Stuart Youth Fund, the Pasadena Arts
& Culture Commission and the City of Pasadena Cultural Affairs Division, the Ahmanson
Foundation, and Sony Pictures Entertainment partially support Red Hen Press.

First Edition
Published by Red Hen Press
www.redhen.org

For Victoria

Contents

1970s

1980s

1990s

2000s

2010s

Psychosis in the Produce Department

1970s

Cancer

This is the disease
of impotence
unclenched fists
smiles frozen
into degeneration

This is the disease
of good girls
who get As
in work habits and cooperation

It is dry ice
smoking from contact
pressed flowers
preserved in the stillness
of their blossoms

It is my grandmother's fear
my mother's acceptance
my structured resignation
to stability

Knives that draw
a fine incision
split regret and dream—
in the halving of my body
is the eagle's flight
and the snail's vision

Defectives

1.

She had an idiot
child
a girl with a Dispose-all
mind
and Barstow eyes
She kept her in the closet
fed her Skippy
$100,000 Dog Food
and brought her out
on Tuesdays
at her bridge party
She always took the last trick
and made a very nice pet.

2.

He had made too many
overtures
flowers
dinners
concerts
He was laughed at
behind his back
He thought he was
Adolphe Menjou.

3.

Phil was a brain
surgeon
He measured everything:
the percentage
in the increase
of his alimony payments,
the number of hairs
that fell from his scalp
He slept 3 1/2 hours
a day
and liked his eggs
scrambled
There was nothing
haphazard about him.

4.

Sylvia was carrying
a paper bag
from Tiffany's
when she stopped by
her Bedford Drive psychiatrist's
for a chat
She discussed
the nature of personal reality

and where to get good juliettes
He gave her a prescription
for 800 mg of Mellaril a day
and 45 minutes of silence.

5.

The 83 bus
went from Wino City
to Santa Monica
The Bag Lady always got
on at Grand
she was into paper—
carried 3 shopping bags
spilling newspaper clippings
Kleenex
26 pencils
crumpled writing paper
and anonymous birthday
cards
On Sundays she unearthed
a yellowed bag
from Saks Fifth Avenue
and sang hymns on her way
to the beach
No one knew her name
but they did know her rank
and Social Security number.

6.

Ron wanted to be
a rock star
He took uppers
and practiced the guitar
He wrote songs
about prepubescent girls
and snorted coke
He formed a band
called Root Canal and decided
to go into dentistry.

7.

In order to maintain
the efficiency
of this machine,
please refer to
The Manual
at all times
The management
disclaims responsibility
for any part or parts
that are defective.

Driving to Laguna

Wanting to speak
but singing and dancing
to Fats Domino
on Dick Clark's salute
to rock and roll
the other two making out
in the back seat
giggling and grabbing
I measure the asphalt
from Buena Park to Irvine
breathe the chilled air
a silver day is the metal in my veins

You are older than me
Beethoven of the cracked hands
working wood and leveling dust
hands that grip around a leather wheel
eyes intent behind black lenses
we cut across to the coast
and ignore the gurgling in the rear
I hum to myself
Do iguanas dance, under the moonlight . . .
songs that make as much sense as we do.

I Coulda Been a Contender

I got it back
pug-scrappy
I almost tossed out
the frenzy and the cockroaches
for a split-level mirage
of dubious companionship

I've been workin' out
I got back
my high school yearbook
I so diligently lent you
because you said you wanted
to see what I looked like
before the nose job
I got back my Gordon Lightfoot
albums I couldn't play
because they weren't hip enough
I got back my dancer's legs
and my depressing poems

I was mainlining insecurity
I was giving up my shot
at the Middleweight Championship of the World
for cheese enchiladas and midnight assignations
I didn't know
that I came so cheap
Meeting you taught me
the meaning of free enterprise

I don't have to barter
for love—I can go the distance
I have got the off-key song
the lopsided smile
and my Ali shuffle
and no amount of Maternal Understanding
is going to make you anything more
than a manipulator of affections
a sparring partner to my heart

I don't need it anymore
I have enough bullshit of my own
than to cope with yours

I got it all back—
the call
the blue-white voltage
the singular identity
I have escaped with my life.

Mary Magdalene
Crosses the Delaware
—for Sharon

Jukebox is crooning
what a fool believes
Ruthie sips a bourbon and seven
she believes
her fool will come
hands filthy with promises
smelling of English Leather
just like the commercials
and the look that says
he's been around
and is just looking
for a good woman like her

I mean, Christ
37 ain't old
I still got all my teeth
I clear 200 a week
in tips

Every week she sizes them up
bikers and handicappers
she reminds them of someone
they knew in Duluth
or Topeka

Ray was different
she could tell
by his smile
that eased past his face

with the charm
of a drunk busted
for vagrancy
his hair was slicked back
real nice
and he talked about big money
big cars
and big women

Honey, what's that you say
about big women?
I've got a chassis like a Cadillac
Coup de Ville
the biggest you ever saw
and a smooth shift
that'll drive you
all the way to Easy Street

How's about we pops the cork
on some Andre bubbly, baby . . .

Sure, Ray said. I was telling
Frank here that this town
could sure use some livening up
and his eyes glittered
and he popped his gum
and sucked his belly in

We could go over to your place
and get better acquainted
he said and put his hand on her
thigh and Ruthie started
to get all wet
and dreams of Whirlpool
washing machines
sang hosannas
from above the bar

It was a quarter of two
and Ruthie knew that if she just
got him home
and he saw the shag rug
he'd want to stay a while
and God she had
corn flakes
and clean sheets

You ain't gonna take advantage
of a nice girl like me?
Me? What you take me for?

They stumbled out of the bar
and up the two flights of stairs
as the moon looked on like a lie detector
behind a smoke screen of clouds.

When a woman starts getting
that hungry look
like Sandra Dee trying
one more beach party
there ain't nobody

that don't see past
a double mick on the stones
and Heaven Sent

But Ray didn't have no place
to spend the night
and he always was a sucker
for red-haired women
and Ruthie knew all the tricks
and licked his earlobe
and touched all those damp
hard places
with varying degrees
of success until
he came
like Macy's Thanksgiving Day Parade
shivering & moaning
like New York in November
and the next day
there was corn flakes
and maybe he did stay
for a while

Or maybe it didn't matter
cause Ruthie changed the sheets
every night
and in the bathroom
was a bottle of English Leather.

Narrow Beds

The spare honest lines
of my girlhood intersect
with wood and linen
Corners neatly tucked
I dreamt alone
with a radio
under my pillow
to ease the nightly terrors
Vampires sucked the dark
Death coaxed slyly
like Southern Comfort

I dreamt alone
long legs became longer
sinew and joint extended
Terror shifted from vertebrae to groin
The womb drummed insistently
Rapists scuttled from street lamps

I hunted boundaries
chanted pregnant lists
of lovers and college lecturers
clocked the seconds
from impulse to scream
slept in sheets of wild control

The demarcation of form—
bed, body, dream—
the weight of cloth
bore me down

There was a limit
a finite space
my body could not slip away.

Rat City

It was a cold night
colder than a lover's eyes
when she tells you
it's no longer good
and Harry
he was just warming up
to some cheap whisky
and a winette
he'd picked up
at Johnny's Shrimp Boat
on 3rd and Main
Saturday night
Saturday night and the boys are out
Saturday night on the edge of a dream in Rat City

So Harry
he got by
sweeping floors
at the Main Street Gym
stealing rubbing alcohol
when things got bad
and he couldn't cop a swig
and he was ready
ready for the night
like a fence for a patsy

He put his hand on Mary's ass
(they were all named Mary)
and says
Baby doncha know I just love ya

and she smiles
like she heard it all before
but it's always the first time
and it's always the last time
and she believes it anyway
cause Harry he has a dream
and a fifth
and it's Saturday night
Saturday night and the boys are out
Saturday night at the edge of a dream in Rat City

Man, there ain't nothing
stopping us
ain't nothing keeping us here
I got vision baby
I got vision clear and simple
there's a place over here
a place I wanna show you
where guys like me
make music to the wind
and blow this town ragged
walk this way honey
I ain't gonna take you
no place you don't wanna go

So Mary she huddles up
real close
and the Mexicans jeer by
laying rubber like a shill turning 21
and blind dogs piss in the street

but Harry he don't see none of it
cause it's Saturday night and the boys are out
Saturday night on the edge of a dream in Rat City

The boys were out
behind the A-1 Factory Shoe Outlet
Russell was there with a sax
he pawned every Monday
blowing sweet like a junkie's promises
and Cal with his horn
that he'd got in Korea
and Harry
he gets out a clarinet
somewhere out of the air
like magic
this one's for you baby
and all that poetry
that's in a man's soul
comes tumbling out
notes tripping over each other
for the pain of it
fire caught on a Saturday night
that you cheat all week for
Saturday night when the boys are out
Saturday night at the edge of a dream in Rat City.

Statuary/Poem for My Girlhood

Four white gazebos corner
a rose garden
out of season
shorn and prickly like a nun
a girl in a white cotton blouse
orange and white polka-dot skirt
winter in California
bare legs and notebook
dry as skin she writes
hollow virginal couplets

In the center stands Apollo
his bronze torso firm and cold
and she knows somewhere
she must reach out
embrace marble to bronze
she buries her face in his plexus
her pale arms encircle
his sturdy legs
and in the coldness of her face
it all comes rushing
the heat of lost art
found in her arms

The Night Grows Teeth

The night grows teeth
needle-visioned
through curtains
under blinds
the women undress
unroll stockings
they sit painting toenails
a subtle mauve

The night grows teeth
a tribal dance
the steady pads
of footfall and drum
he stands at the window
chest bare
to listen
she circles his back
the night grows teeth
with soft sucking kisses
he unclasps her beads

Grit-song
clench-song
the night grows teeth
it lurches like a madman
it holds you down
it silences you with its heavy hands
it opens you up with its hot breath
it dares you to dream

I know about the night
I whistle myself into waking
I've fashioned arrowheads
from stone
the night grows teeth
it demands retribution
leather straps
and burnt flesh
horsehide
batwing
I paint my face
with yellow ochre
I carry a knife between my teeth.

The Red Pencil

Cancels
documents
lists our stealthy regrets
the last rites of bitterness
tart wild apples
trappings from another burial,
from an enchantment like sleep
encasing a beauty suspended
in blush and inviolate.

Long before princes,
I remember this:
that purity is lost with experience
that regret is a grey killer
more terminal than folly.

My fingers still close
around red pencils
still move blindly
across paper
canceling time and recrimination
like an exile returning without baggage.

Three Years Later I Still Send Anonymous Postcards to You

3 years gone
I scrawl a message
30,000 happy New Mexicans greet you
you never took me
seriously
my 1966 Buick
my Gene Wilder fan club card
my famous Los Angeles poet t-shirt

but let me tell you this
I have lived for you
each month
as on the 17th I write
having time here
wish you were wonderful
messages written with blood
as each month I send
a jagged fragment
of some ill-conceived dream
that finished my girlhood as swiftly
as my parents' bedroom door locked
at midnight

it is all done with precision
red print on white card
I choose deliberately
Roy Rogers on Trigger
a fitting tribute
to another outlaw
I want to say

that it doesn't matter—
this vigil—
but when you pace hallways
holding on against a fear
you cannot name
a fear
that shakes you
from your sleep
only to realize you were awake
all along—
then you know it does matter
it matters that once
each month
there is the memory
of something as tenuous
as a possibility
as real as this poem

Travesty

Wings beating
against stone—
what we do
to each other
in the name
of love
is splattered
against walls
on civilized
streets.

27 Years of Madness

1.

It is always there—
it is in the steak knife
you run across your palm
to see
just to see
if you will bleed
it is in the face
in the mirror
you want to smash
for telling you lies
the eyes for falsifying beauty
the mouth for voicing fraud
the ears that were prey to every con man

2.

I used to believe
it was natural to sing
in elevators
just like Fred Astaire
did it—then so did I
until at 17
Mama said
don't you know only crazy
people sing in elevators

3.

And then there was Jasper
rattling around
where no one could see him
a whisper behind
my left ear
and I would
cut cut cut
on my arms to show him
I was sincere
and rip rip rip
open my stomach
to show him
I was pure
virginal
wanting his unborn children

And they called this madness?
I was as eager
as any House and Garden bride

4.

The hospitals were clever

They said: you have the gift
why do you want to destroy it?
And I will tell you now

it is not a gift
to know that words are not your own
to know you can produce
a prism from nothingness
it is a terror to be a magician—
that somebody who lives in this body
and I who never wanted this body
becomes
Good Laurel
Darling Laurel
Gifted Laurel

These are all names
they name me
they strip my controls
they open the skull
and peer inside
not knowing that I
have the final control of my life

I can destroy it

5.

James and Ramon were fighting
in the day room
the orderlies rushed in
they were separated
blood on the walls

someone walks me
back to my room
I turn my head
they leave the room
I open the drawers
I take out my stockings
I am not there
I take the chair
I go to the bathroom
I stand on the chair
I knot the stockings around my neck
I knot the other end to the shower rod

I really am your good girl mama

Union Station

I needed a timetable
for my heart
it always arrived
too early
departed too late
wandered lost on platforms

I needed you
to steamroller the creases
I folded too many times
I was hurry and drag
beat slow
sync steps

I came in pieces
like cartons tied
with baling wire
you held tight
against the spillage
and random punches

Oh I loved you like speed
like fast exits
and jackrabbit starts

you held all the tickets
you opened the gates

it was 2 minutes to boarding
and we pulled out all the stops

1980s

A Little Death

each evening
before twilight
before starlight
before the yellow houses
pull their shutters
into themselves

I remember my own
small death
in green and orange
and ash white pills
each beautiful
each perfect
each swaddling my senses
in cotton batting
and antiseptic truth
junkie truth

I have died
these many familiar times
this comfort
pulls my life about me
with sleepy fingers
like a warm blanket
and rocks me
with soft lullabies

no mother could
ever be so diligent
so real
so mine

one
two
buckle my shoe

twenty years
of little deaths
have left me
silent and barren
as Mother Sleep
no longer waits for me
drawing a tepid bath
but instead
opens her starched white uniform
and smothers me in her ample arms.

A Poem for Brian

They were thick, hypnotic days
driving through towns
with names like Castroville.
Me and Brian fighting over comic books
in the back seat of a 1956 Packard.
He was on my side of the invisible line
drinking warm Orange Crush.
I lost Salinas to idle revenge.

I was always the smart one,
the one who stayed out of trouble.
I lived in books until I was 20.

There are no lines now
or maps charting
where we've been.
You've grown up sturdy.
My days run thin like a current.

Come home, come home.
In your voice is a history
of cramped summers
and towns with exotic museums.
You stand rooted
with muscle, with grunt.
I cross foreign boundaries
of Army, wife and asphalt
to call you
Brother.

All the Earnest Young Men

At night he drives a taxi
and reads Kerouac
and in 1967
1984
2003
the song is still the same
the answer is blowing in the wind

His lips believe everything he says,
the kisses and philosophy,
voice above acoustic guitar.
"Must" and "now" and "change"
flush his face like seasons

I trace the brow that will furrow,
the jaw that will set,
with sad fingers roughened
from Innocent to Older Woman
and want to hold him there forever,
my daphne flower,
until I see him again
marching for honor
disappearing in weary streets.

Chiropractor of Love

He was available for house calls
and she could feel her spine
when he cracked her she was silly putty
until she was stretched out
and gooey
and that wasn't all
he was cheap
cheaper than her gynecologist anyway
he gave her life meaning
he gave her a standing appointment
soon she began to hum
a low vibrato in her chest

DETECTIVE SUPREMO

L.A. Bogen, Detective Supremo.

My very name
rolls on the tongue
like an aperitif
or a recalled cheese
an open parenthesis of mayhem
on the make
in the sulky afternoon
of Los Angeles
clues burn rubber
at my touch (again)
you say
you want something
black and lethal
and smoking

I remember the *Dain Curse Case*
and smooth the seams
on black silk stockings

Baby, what you need
is a little private surveillance
a little Mickey Finn
night on the town
a 1-2 combination

You forget a smile
as I tap red
lacquer nails on glass

and exhale
a Santa Ana condition
Mulholland Drive
and the whole bloody San Andreas Fault

And suddenly
the bougainvillea greet you
like a happy extortionist

and it's Cinco de Mayo
everywhere you look
as I melt into crowds
just one step behind you.

DETECTIVE SUPREMO
MEETS HER MATCH

It began as a clandestine affair
too hot not to cool down
and I'm not talking centigrade
we were stumbling in hotels
discovering each other like penicillin
still, when the heart sputters
everyone is suspect
even you
after a month
as amiable and dapper
as Nick Charles without a hangover
while I rummage through your purloined past
for the stink of duplicity
sure I'm paranoid
but I'm paid to be
checking for fingerprints
a useful disguise in any event

I consult the stars
old men and bookies
they all say the same thing

Keep straight and carry a light bulb

You arrive at my doorstep
Silver bullet roses
and a 200-watt glint in your eyes.

HAVANA

Damp gardenias pause
this night Havana
your name a sigh
rolled on the thighs
of bronze women
Istanbul, Cairo
were discarded
like petals
this is my season of Havana

Once I held a black ink pen
and wrote a word
I scarcely knew
H   you emerged unsettled
a   with each letter
v   followed this day's vivid streets
a   to find me here
n   it is for you I paint my lips coral
a   it is for you

Havana, you lick into corners
of the red night
drunk on Cuba Libres
and sugar cane water
tango, samba
the scratch of phonograph
beguiles the blood
to begin the tissuing off
of taffeta, corset, stockings
you move against me

your face a muzzle, a gun
the circular fan clicks seconds
te amo your black curls
shake and my head shakes
Yes

We rise from ashes of the night
dress and leave
we do this again and again
Havana, you are all
they warned me about:
more than the sum
of my self and my others
more than that, more
you are every drug, liquor and sin
that was whispered among young girls
and still I choose you

You take me down pungent streets
this is the street of orchids
where you wooed me
with ambiguous dilemmas
this is the street of hibiscus
where I sweep my hair away
from my face and memorize
lips tangled in strands
here are mango, indigo, papaya
slow streets that move
like sweet intoxication
until your tattoo appears

on my shoulder
and the stretch of our bodies
pads like cats the curve
from waist to hip
the round of belly
the knowledge of muscle

Must I divulge my secrets?

This is Hard Time, Havana
a time when the wind blows black
and your name appears on a park bench
you beckon
from the smokestacks of Pittsburgh
and the windowsills of Manchester
and are gone

I took you home
folded you away
a bureau
where your name breathes
a hot wind blowing Havana

I Eat Lunch with a Schizophrenic

I check for Gestapo agents
under the table.
There are no electronic bugs
in the flowers.
We talk freely
about jamming devices
and daredevil escapes.
The waitress asks
if everything is OK,
I tell her fine
except for the two SS officers
sitting drinking Rob Roys
pretending not to watch us.
They slip a secret message
on the check—
Please Pay When Served.
Dollars or marks
I ask.
She says just pay up
and spits out her gum
on the napkin.
Her name tag says Barbi.
I don't want to make a scene
so I pay the bill
and glance at my jr. hypnotist watch.
Large segments
of the world's population
have been converted by this time
saving machine
I strap to my wrist

disguised as a Timex.
I turn it on the SS officers.
They think nothing's changed
but we know different.

We know the allies
are going to bust
in here with tear gas
and submachine guns
looking for Nazi Jew-haters.

The problem's not in the hamburgers
chili
or cokes
I explain
the problem is in being susceptible.

In Praise of Spinsters

I am as bountiful as corn
my face turned towards the sun
I sing in praise of spinsters
who weave their hair
to make strong rope
who cast their dreams
to make fine pots
we are your mystery
the ones who slipped away
I celebrate what we are
clay sifting through fingers
women alone
harvesting the earth

LIVE STEAM AT 8:45

In this poem there are no words
all language has stopped
but the pumps boil
live steam
live steam
live steam at 8:45

Hearts poach/we rip at skin
alone and without noise
to get at the beat
the color
and where the words are
but this is a poem
where there are no words
and all the colors are extinct
rising like steam
that hisses in our throats
like wordless lies

In this poem the words sizzle
and evaporate

In this poem the words rise crazy

In this poem our bodies ache
our fingers can murder us
but even though we fear death
we offer ourselves to each other
as if the muscle and breath
of our bodies can also heal

This poem cradles in its palm
those things that cannot be said

It asks that you touch this page.

MAY 12, 1971

Mornings starch white
the rumple of pastel sheets
two figures angle
and stave off encroachment
the sun blinks above canisters
bodies snap to attention

they move without collision
smooth and defined
collars and buttons contain static

it is 7:34
a Wednesday

the figures compact themselves in chairs
there is coffee and stock reports
it is cheery like this
the day propped before them
like the Wall Street Journal

the solidity and logic
of the counter is interrupted
only by a wedding band
in the soap dish
and a pair of scissors
to cut coupons out of skin

she says she has to do something
he says that would be nice
and his vacant sky falls to linoleum

the short breath of morning
bustles questions into kitchen corners
it pats the figures on their hands
and says "there, there dear, it's all right."

ONE

Love is a penalty. We are punished
for not having been able to stay alone.
—Marguerite Yourcenar

What is this need to refuse
that punctuates the seamless hours
and separates yes into no?
A faint wind,
it prefers itself,
the madwoman you are afraid
to invite to dinner.

Quietly you pace your spinster days.
Morning glories choke the lintel.
You look for your kind
in that exile,
in that banished exile of solitude.
You cannot stay alone like this,
facing a reflection of your face
you reach out
and stumble into your own arms.

ORIGAMI: THE UNFOLDING HEART

I beat a stillness
of blue tissue birds
from shreds
learning to fold
smooth
chrysanthemums
gold and violet
colors run deep
as solitude

Mine was the loneliness
of comets
so high
and untouchable
that only the most
foolhardy
dared follow
the brilliance
of my tail
that singular shiver
a hollow consummation
I could not hold

for the tearing
of hearts
no longer muscle
a sheer tissue
I learned to fold
again
my body circling

legs around waist
arms against chest
and these gentle birds
flutter wings
heart and heart

Orpheus Ascended
(Homage to Orwell)

a blue note floats
over the city
settles like a sob
in his throat
he had thought himself
singularly extraordinary
wild strawberries in November
or black gardenias on a doorstep

pride is the strength
of losers
mr. no dice
mr. see you later
his collar turned
against the wind
the wind that whistles his transgressions
in a city where transgressions
hopscotch and multiply
in predictable patterns
and now the brick wall
of his own building rises
resolutely
slammed with posters

Part of This Is True, But I Forget Which Part

I sat in a chair
there were large red roses
a pattern
like others he said
most distressing
like waking up
dead
serious condition
he reached inside
my chest
it was wet and slippery there
were large red roses
on the table
a man's brush
lips/cheek
my eyes flowered
everything fat and red
like legs sticky
with rote patterns
a serious condition
can be alleviated

Psychosis in the Produce Department

It is all
too much
squish.
Tomatoes
leer
rub red
against the flesh.
There is danger
in their eyes
as the carts
chart collision courses.

Killers are everywhere,
mushrooms disguise as evolution.

I keep the juices intact,
encased in animal skin.
We pick our food
for ripeness and color.
The cucumbers smirk
and beckon.
My veins pop
like grapes between fingers.
I wheel metal
through bins.

Pigmy Headhunters and Killer Apes, My Lover and Me

Pigmy headhunters and killer apes play basketball at the Y. The killer apes win but the pigmy headhunters are not sore losers. They take the basketball home and boil it in your cast iron pot.

Hair. Lots of hair. Hairy devils those pigmy headhunters and killer apes. Vidal Sassoon chewed on this dilemma for a while.

Pigmy headhunters and killer apes had flannel cakes at Musso and Frank's. They were very hungry and ate three helpings each. But they wondered about the flesh beneath my flannel.

Pigmy headhunters and killer apes were homesick for Africa. They watched Make Mine Malt-O-Meal on TV. They especially liked the part where Paul saved the world with gruel. It reminded everyone of home and they all had a good cry.

A cup of coffee is an honest thing. More honest than I am now. Its velocity in my veins throbs with need. I need to tell you this. You make my head hurt like sutures. You make my silly fist a killer.

Bone, hair, water, food. It is morning again. Last night the jungle used my fractured jaws to spear a message. Pigmy headhunters dance while killer apes beat their chest forget about you forget about you forget about you.

The Day I Had the Terrible Fear

The Big No sits on my chest
and I think I'm only 36
but the invitation remains
Hi ya How ya doin?
have some coffee and some pie
have a serrated bread knife!

I cannot name it yet
it squanders my daylight
black familiar coin
of the psycho trade
I remember it each time
it leaves me crouched
and flinching
still I brazen
fate and furies after a fashion
The Big No is indiscriminate
it doesn't care that I'm a Famous Los Angeles Poet
it will erode everything
it takes away the words, man
it takes away the words

The Illuminati Projects

1. Mom and the Goldfish

This be the story of Mom. This be the story of Mom. This be the story of Mom she have the magenta hair. She have the glass eye and the Tupperware smile. She have the look of the man who eat razor blade and live.

Mom she live in the Projects. This Project she call Cram 'Em Up Old Timers. 5,327,060 Old Timer in 2 block. Mom she be the youngest Old Timer in the block be a snappy 71. The Old Timers they play Parcheesi and Canasta on the stoop many long hours. They not play with Mom because Mom she have the Hidden Dice in the false teeth and the Ace Up the Sleeve.

So Mom she sit at home and knit the three arm sweater. She defrost the ice box many long day. She watch the rerun of *Get Smart* and say she already is. She talk on phone to cousin the Seattle.

She say if only I had the friend with the oily walk and the Hallelujah Chorus on his mind, I be so happy she say. She say this many long day to herself and to others. No one listen.

One day she unroll pink foam hair curler from head. She hear gasp ". . . King of Kings and Lord of Lords" a cappella from sidewalk.

It be Nathan Goldfish. Nathan Goldfish be six foot mother with monocle and walking stick. He don't need no tails. He got fins, baby. He come from uptown where he live in bathtub of wealthy suburbanite cum actress who use him for immoral purposes. She throw him out when he discover Jesus.

Now he flip-flop on street half dead/half crazy a-singing of Jesus and rattling pencil cup. He say "Alms for the Poor." He say "Keep Young Fish Off the Street."

Mom she know a sucker when she see one.

"Come in Sonny, I show you my etchings and nurse you back to health."

Nathan he grateful. Nathan he thank the Lord. Nathan he throw down pencil cup and slither on belly to stoop.

Inside he lay on plastic covered sofa and look at curious turquoise flowers made from bird feathers. Mom she put on Liberace to sooth the savage sole and make the chicken soup.

Mom be good mom. Mom nurse Nathan Goldfish with cold compresses and mercurochrome. Mom sing the lullaby. Mom show baby pictures of Mom.

Nathan he get better. He start to sing "Satisfaction" and "Love Minus Zero No Limit." He be slightly out of hip date.

He say I need to spread fins. He say I need to swim my way across USA bathtub to bathtub. He say Mom I love your puce (by now it was) hair and your cackle when you walk. I see you around like a doughnut.

But Mom she ain't going to give up her good thing. She already wore out 1 Liberace, 3 Burt Bacharach, 4 KC and Sunshine Band records. She already beat him 12 games Scrabble, 2 games Monopoly, 1 game Strip Poker. She discover the secret recipe for kelp loaf and algae burgers.

She make plan.

She put Crazy Glue in bathtub.

Nathan Goldfish he lay down in tub for pause that refreshes. But he don't get up. He stuck.

Mom she say "Who gonna leave now pretty baby?" She hit Nathan Goldfish with frying pan. She cut fin with butcher knife. She tape eyeball close. She read him the collected works of Rod McKuen.

Nathan he helpless. Nathan he sick and cry out.

Mom she say, "sing the Hallelujah Chorus, sonny boy."

Mom she say, "shut up and deal."

2. Love of Shoe

Oh love of shoe. He have love of shoe. White bucks. Black pumps. Shoes for peace. Shoes for industry.

He watch shoe of women walking to work. He love the secretary shoe. The shoe have the good sense. It bet on Native Dancer. It play the shoe horn. The shoe be no-nonsense.

He love the no-nonsense shoe. It know when to put the foot down. It be up-front. It stand on own two feet. It wear the eyeglasses and go to Vassar on scholarship.

No-nonsense shoe have the degree in art history and work in the insurance agency. Oh he want to free her to dance the light fantastic. He want to show her the Tintoretto.

Oh the shoe. The love of shoe that stumble when she hurt when she lose the dream. She want the rhinestone clip-ons and the spike heel. She want the staccato of her heel in the Spanish cabaret, the taffeta skirt at the ankle, the eye on the foot.

Yes. Yes.
Yes.
He take her home. He clean the kitchen. He empty the ash tray. He straighten the sheet and the pillowcase.

This be it.

He take her to the exclusive salon. The polish. The stream line. The work up whittle down like the 35-year old divorcee from Palm Springs.

He make the satin curtain. He make the fur rug for her to sleep. Oh the love of shoe!

Boot servant. I be your boot servant. I love your thin hot spikes. Walk on my chest.

He take off the glasses. She throw back the chair. He rip off the shirt. She get out the black gloves.

Walk on my chest.

She grind her pointed black toe on the sternum. He gasp with pain.

Tell me what it feel to be ugly. The no-nonsense shoe. The shoe with no magic. Tell me how I give you magic.

I love to see you moan. She hiss. I kick you in the face. I owe you everything. I devour you. I walk on your chest.

Oh the shoe

Oh the shoe

Oh the love of shoe

Oh the love of shoe oh

Oh the love of shoe oh

Oh

Oh

Oh

OOOhh The Tintorettos. The Botticellis. The dainty dreams of the art history major.

The ivory tower. The Rapunzel Complex.

She learn the power that undo the laces. She kick out the jams. She light the candle and she know the curse.

Daily he falls in love of shoe. They line the closet in the neat row. They be separate by color and date. He know the mission. He liberate the shoe from the constraints of conventional morality. He understand their baseness. It be OK.

3. Gene Wilder Saved My Life (Woman Tells All)

yes it be true he did he really did swear to god things be pretty bad you know the
heart be pumping tears and there be no stopping it any of it at all the work be too
rock hard what I got to show for any of it and no stopping but keep going can't
look over my shoulder or know they be taking it all away whatever it be I want it
all to stop or did but now maybe just to be and why can't I have it all anyway you
know about Gene Wilder who be the love of the life 16 time I see Silver Streak
sit through 12 hour Gene Wilder marathon and no getting up to pee even every
single Gene Wilder movie ever made I see at least 5 time except the *Saturday
Game* which I miss on TV and never found the rerun I just can't stand it no more
I say I want out of this mess no man who want me hell I be no dummy and maybe
I be not pretty but don't crack no mirrors and where be the money this got to stop
got to sleep got to sleep so I don't wake up and Gene Wilder maybe he be just a
dream like this nightmare place be twisted in my heart no more pain forever no
more this be it and even though I promise in my heart to go tomorrow the first
show the first day Gene Wilder *The World's Greatest Lover* my heart say no more
I took the whole thing I know what you be thinking but I just be so tired that I
took the whole thing and there be no puking even though I don't drink normal
and there be that whole bottle gin too it be thick in the ear fall down a lot I can't
stop run some more it buzz and heart heart heart just sleep please forever I say
when the eyes open not well I see blur and spin the legs not work so good pissed as
hell that it not work and there be no more pills in the goddamn bottle and no only
that I miss the first show the first day Gene Wilder *The World's Greatest Lover*
what the hell nothing else doing anyway maybe he forgive it only be the third
show so I call Danya say Gene Wilder at 4 pm OK she say we take the bus with
no lines anywhere not even on my face this be a joke except I look like shit and I
be standing in line at the movies Danya be holding me up I not stand so good you
know I hear a voice would you let me step in front of you miss I want to see the

audience eyes focus on blue shirt shoes eyes and my heart stop right there oh god it be him oh god I cry fall down weep at the enormity of everything quiet I love you Mr. Wilder I love you oh god you save my life I cry alone if I be dead I never see you the world's greatest lover I never understand we all must hold tight above all unchain heart.

4. *The Singing Telegram*

LA-LA. GOOD NEWS FOR YOU. STOP. LOVE. STOP. LOVE STOP. LA-LA. SINGING IN SHOWER. HE WAS. LA-LA. RAIN ALWAYS YOU THINK. SHOWERS. BABIES. GOOD NEWS FOR YOU. STOP. THE SUN. SHINING AGAIN. STOP. NO RAIN. LA-LA. TOMORROW BABIES AND PROMISES. STOP. TOMORROW. LA-LA. HE WAS. STOP. THE MOST IN THE WORLD. OF EVERYTHING YOU LOVE. LA-LA. SING SING SING ECHOING AGAINST TILE. ABANDONED PRISON. LATER YOU WOULD SPEAK. STOP. A GLASS WALL BETWEEN YOU. STOP. YOU WANT TO SMASH. GOOD NEWS FOR YOU. YOU SAY STOP. LOVE. I LOVE. STOP. SMASH WALLS HE SINGS IN SHOWER *BREAK ON THROUGH TO THE OTHER SIDE*. STRANGE CONCERT. YOUR SEATS WERE ON THE SIDE. SIDE LINES. YOU NEVER SPOKE DIRECTLY. STOP. GUARDED EVERYWHERE. STOP. HIDING EVERYWHERE. STOP. YOU GO UPSTAIRS LA-LA. BREAK ON THROUGH TO THE OTHER SIDE. SPLATTER SPLATTER-SPLATTER ON TILE. STOP. KNOCK KNOCK. HE IS THE THING. STOP. MORE THAN ANY SECRET. MORE THAN YOUR FIRST TREASURE: YOUR GRANDMOTHER'S RING. MORE THAN MEMORY. SHOWERS AND PROMISES TOO LOUD/NOT LOUD ENOUGH. STOP. KNOCK KNOCK. LA-LA. A QUIET STOPPING MOMENT. YOUR HEART IS KNOCK KNOCK. THE DOOR OPENS. INSIDE EVERY. THING. SHINES. HE IS MORE THAN YOUR FIRST KISS. MORE THAN YOUR EIGHTH GRADE SCIENCE PROJECT. HE STANDS WET AND SHINING. STOP. YOU SING. STOP. GOOD NEWS FOR YOU. STOP. I LOVE. STOP. YOU. STOP.

The Möbius Strip

A blue spot
and saxophone
a cramped haze
she darts brittle
eyes too quick to sparkle
jaw clenched smile
the sax winds slow
her eyes half close

Oh mama the laugh
too sharp to hush
it pierces
like the remembering
that peels the dress-up
like mama
like fairy princess clothes
she lets fall
a plume
some bird of paradise
dreams

She remembers dancing
and Shanghai Cyd Charisse
smoky legs wrapped around
Gene Kelly snaking "gotta dance"
she had wanted
never to stop
leave the theater dancing
so hard
there ought to be a law

She used to say
we are all dancers
all pulse and sound
we're all we need to know
a quickening beyond shadows
that flies through walls
windows
wails like a truth
so beautiful and real
that your heart could crack

She grinds out
beginnings and endings
tragic gardenias
the present turns back
on itself and becomes future
and the sax
mournful and low
sings lullabies and elegies

THE POWER LINES
ARE DOWN

Current spilling into current
I am cross-wired
aborted energy
mad with voltage
I flash neon signals

Love me
you

Fool
I spill all crazy
the fusion
of teashops and suicides
coming and going
without shieldings

Meltdown
meltdown
whalebone and garter
I will not be confined
by steel casings
or wedding rings
my name is preceded
by a warning—
the power lines are down
love me

The Room

It is large enough
for the secret you cannot forget
a hot plate and our pull-down bed.
This room hovers over walls
that are as transparent
as well-meaning fabrications—
I never promised
you the truth here
only this room.
Come, here's the key
a wisp of memory
caught in your hair

Outside this room:
intangible buildings vanish
days disappear
a new landlord
knocks on the door
demanding rent past due
as we huddle in overcoats
knowing that this fragile warmth
opens the windows
opens the door

THE VIRGINIA WOOLF GUIDE TO ROCK COLLECTING

Small hard pebbles can be as effective as rough boulders. They may lodge unobtrusively in kidneys and gall bladders. If deemed necessary, their growth may be accelerated through gastric intake.

He sat in the alley behind the house in Santa Monica where he lived with his parents. Birds screamed in his ears. A striped yellow cat rubbed his leg hungrily. It growled deep and throaty. The boy found a stone in his hand. He judged it to be of the right dimension and weight as he smashed it again as he smashed it again as he smashed it again on the yellow cat's head.

She said that it was too hard. He had left her heart jagged and cleft like a stone artifact. She was rock and he had made her cold. He had made her cold.

Virginia Woolf stooped pearl grey and dun against the sea. She gathered stone children to her breasts. She tucked them in pockets like secrets. Face like slate, she straightened and walked into the waves.

Trio

1.

Her belly grows larger
yesterday it was a bundt pan
Pride and Prejudice
snapshots from Mexico.
Today it is layaway
a 1980 Kenmore washer and dryer
and yellow plastic pacifiers.

It wants to be the moon,
a mango you sink
your face into.
You get lost in her fullness
and kiss her pomegranate lips.
Now she winds her fine hair
around your throat and fingers,
she pulls you inside her
and weaves your future
like a knot.

2.

The book says
you have to learn
how to breathe.
You learn together,
going with the pain.
Your long ohhhh's

glide like notes
on Tuesday mornings
and Thursday afternoons
when I would sing
Falling in love again
never wanted to
what am I to do
can't help it.

Untitled L.A. Poem

The palms flatten
against chance hot winds
we bore in for the duration
rigid
even the palms yield
to our touch
oh Los Angeles
we are your spawn
whim and hope
our eyes pan
one another
for the right side
the solid profile

Your face screens huge
I cannot reach behind
for the yes
the hungry yes
we need so much
we cannot even touch
the palms
of our hands
tight fists
we hold it in
we hold it in

VICTORIA

The first things you see
are the plants
trailing spiked leaves
down bookshelves
climbing to precarious heights
like foolish children
she calls them by name
to soothe their captive souls

We talk of lost secret things
the movement of stars
the shift and grasp of seasons
how we remember the pristine
houses of our girlhoods

Her hands turn soil
with long white fingers
she cleaves a shoot
nestles it in adobe
and offers it like a confidence

green is the color of love

VULNERABLE STREET

You have no idea
but gear and shift
engine ramming the dark
the moon has no lock
as you race down Vulnerable Street

in the twilight
your hair flies like an exclamation
forgive me it wails
such consideration
is the stuff of barricades
the cinderblocks I stack
one by one
against you

You Pirate You

Those as hunts treasure must go alone, at
night, and when they find it they have to
leave a little of their blood behind them.
—Loren Eiseley

Alone I sniffed
for buried treasure
the tumble of night
in your wandering eye.

I chose you
for your swagger
and cutlass tongue
I did not mind
the lash you left there.

Tattoo that is your name
more precious than gold doubloons.
I scratch the letters on my arm.
The ink and blood still mix.

1990s

ALSO FRANKENSTEIN

Because he was mine the thing I'd made
screamed when he felt the light . . .
—Lawrence Raab

Behemoth I called him
he, too, was mine
clumsy and large
oddly endearing.
He wanted so to please me
brought me crystal and tissue
it was all the same to him
gifts from the Magi
or coffee filters

I wanted more
from my own creation—
was that wrong?
I wanted the stellar
and black cosmos
I wanted illusion
I wanted—
dare I say it—
devotion . . .

Certainly he was devoted
he had no choice
I filled his hours
with marvels of my humanity
his rooms with my grandiose longing

But he wasn't content
with my mythology
my reasoning
the folly of Icarus
flew before me

Still I gave in
I opened the thin edge
of the wedge
stood before him
trembling and radiant
I reached inside my chest
here is where it burns
and *here*
and *here*

My thin hands
held that cold pale light
it glittered with a blue flame
and flecked with ice.

(Avalanche)

(my secret name)

frozen tundra glints
in moonlight
as precise
         as this
                  icicle
while fault lines slash
dissident crags into mountains
and the Gestapo
waits outside the window
in the snow
with its dogs

(will you say it?)

BLUE SMOKE AND STEEL

All nerve, this city
ferocious, it chews
and spits out
exhales blue
smoke and steel
and I am like this city
edging towards oblivion
the mirror cuts whatever facts
I have known about myself
woman/artist a quick fix
this identity a hook
to pin my nightclothes on

What do I know about reality?
celluloid captures my tinsel and frailties
as I jag through barrios and suburbs
mini-malls pock the landscape

Los Angeles, mi corazón
what has become of you?

I remember fruit trees
blossoming like my dreams
of success now uprooted
by a concrete depression
we work
we wait
nothing comes
not synapse, sex or sacrament

just the toil of the mundane
overblown by expectation
as it budges like a cancer
with no chance of remission

we go to bed at night
we get up in the morning
again and again and again

BONES DIG THIS DREAM

she knew it
couldn't explain it
followed her great
yearning for bones
tibia
femur
phalange
cut her teeth
on bones
bones dig grave
thirteenth hour yips
dead leaves at her feet

marrow root she hisses
more than skin
she digs deeper
kneads and massages
until she feels bone
    NOW
O Grave Undertaker
root of this dream
be bone
be marrow
be what you mean

COLD, COLD, COLD

I am your mushroom daughter
pallid and fecund
blooming in the night
my etched face
in the window
forever an accusation

yes, I have stood
at the foot of the table
and refused nourishment
as you, Mother Lampshade
held the court
of Sick-Unto-Death
a nightly ritual
grounded in the cresting moon

ice within fire

I deny all charges
brought against me
that I longed for life
betrayed your honor
danced on your bloody fields

our cancerous spores
my mushroom life
glow incandescent
                    even now
my sisters and I encircle you
in your jagged tooth pathology

we excise

ice within fire

Sick-Unto-Death

Fission

1.

Of neurons singing
pharmaceutical jazz
I am chemically altered
thank you Eli Lilly
and my esteemed contagion
of AMA-approved psychiatric professionals

Did I say Out Of My Mind?

Hogtied to a delicate imbalance
dropperful of clarity
pale liquid appropriate
for the condition

Oh what am I to do?
Do do do

What am I to do
when my mind turns screws
of apocrypha
into failsafe truths?

The way a face just sets
concerned and distant
while I babble and babble
I can't take this
I won't stand that

My face frightens me
purple and loud
I would not want to know her

2.

The girl called herself
Diana Nightingale
Diana Frecklewitz Nightingale
laughed her parents
trying to make her stop
wanting to be someone else

3.

I am the sun
of all
my experience,
insight
interaction with life

4.

My maternal grandmother
Sarah Eva Ely Ramsay Walser
with her Hudson seal coat
and straight straight seams

smoking Kools
down to the filters
taught me the finer ice picks
of womanhood

Saturdays, when my brother
went to track meets with Dad
she and I
and usually my mother
had tea at the Bullock's Wilshire
Tea Room where I chewed
and swallowed cinnamon toast
and an endless parade
of crustless petite sandwiches
with white cotton gloves
in my lap
chic blonde women
like my mother
dreaming of Grace Kelly
stopped by our table
modeling St. John knits
or black and pink Chanel suits
whispering "This can be found
in the French Room
on the second floor"

My nose was too big
my hair too brown
and curly for the place
with its watered silk drapes

and rose-strewn carpet
the chicken salad
and tomato aspic
"But she has such nice
posture, don't you think?"
my mother, ever the WASP
would say
smoothing the pink organza
on my spun glass dress

"Helen, the child is perfect—
I'll take her if you can't
get a hold of yourself
and that Other Girl of yours.
Dominion over the primitive
in all our lives is the Jesus
Principle. She's a good girl,
aren't you darling, she looks
just like me, I told her we
could be twins"

And I chewed and chewed
but did not dip my toast
in the hot chocolate, a lady
I did not spot the dress
I could wear ten times
before it was washed

My grandfather
Frederick Ramsay
my mother's father
committed suicide
when she was seven
some say because
of the Depression
and no work
some say because of
Sarah Eva Ely Ramsay Walser
and fear

5.

I guess you could say
I know a lot about fear
knucklebone and murder
in my own bed
fear of failing and falling

6.

Funny how failure and falling
sound alike—the firings failing
and falling pling pling pling
in my brain
my managed care brain
my climate control brain

That friction and fission
sound alike is funny
this friction and fiction
sound alike, ha-ha

7.

The friction of my life
against my life is my life

8.

The fission of my life
despite my life is my life.

Guilt

slams its head up like a fist
like your first menstruation
a surgical tongue
yapping sainthood or death
a scab to be pulled off
this humanity is all clotted

the first thing you don't remember
returns holding you hostage
a switchblade at your throat
tell the truth, isn't this fun
a trip to the sea or better yet
immortality blinks in the night
what is this thing
what is it
waving you down
with a pale handkerchief
it gets in and drives you on
off the road
grabbing you where thought comes from

Harvest Come Home

My father sits huddled
in his winter mind
stubble and chill
have aged him
I gather him in
to skirts as full
as I am—no longer a girl
but willow strong
gathering all my pretty
ones: poems and dreams

I call out father
who was oak
father who was tree
I reach for you
with twigs and nestlings
small gray doves to sing
in your branches

I billow my skirts
and send them flying
up up up
through your spare hours
your brittle leaves
you, whose song turns
back on itself and chokes
mute and stammering

Harvest I say
harvest come home
there is plenty for you here

Homestead

Her hands clip the air
he calibrates the weeds
they had planned a victory garden
a monument to their undying
love one
two
three
steps to the porch
a dog in a cage
tears at metal
too fierce for propriety

do you want to know
what they dream about?
the moon-pulled waves of Easter Island
a pan of milk lapping at their toes

they pull up weed and root
babies fatten like tubers underground
dropped into haphazard baskets
with their trowels, snails and fruit

they inch slowly forward
soon
soon they think
looking to the clouds
soon we will be
so very happy

Hope Leaps from Her Chair

Time fries the noodle
all of which goes and goes
thoughtless in a white room
in a headful of wires
copper kitchen of family

this little piggy goes to market
fat neck to chopping board
a mother who slices and dices
and Hope flees the room
does not reappear like the Virgin Mary
on a fire escape

I pull the switch
and wait across the table
an electric blender
churning for 42 years
I wait, I switch, I wait

LAST EXIT TO EAST JESUS

We've come from Racine,
Tacoma, East Lansing.
We've come to discover
whatever meaning we can
in our godforsaken backyards
in our barbecues and swing sets.

Square rooms opening
on other square rooms,
endless fields of opportunity
flatten in our daily aperture
of truncated dreams.
6 p.m. and we roll out
from dinner, shambling, put-
our-hands-on-the-television-set
and say THANK YOU

JESUS, who died and was resurrected
in the morning paper for our sins
and we are so grateful
for smallness of it all
minutia elevated to grace.
We hold our truths to be self-evident
schedule and dictum guide
or circumspect journeys.

The last exit to East Jesus.
We took the turnpike south
and didn't stop until we got here.

Morning Fever 11 a.m.

A way station shimmers
in the distance
Nurse Health beckons
with cold compresses
and gingerly I follow
spit on the ground
and say what the hell
I'm back for another round
of ticketing and calibration

this time I walk away
from the Dark Conductor
who nods and whispers
another ride for us, my friend
chill and sweat erupt
as he passes by my chair
and I remember my appointment
in deathly pale Samara

the visible heat wavers
in the livid interior—
a bruise of palm and aqua—
and at the depot
street vendors offer me oranges

I want a cigarette
a thin steel razor

Myopia

To commence with fact:
you are, of course,
a crusted pox
on humanity
a complete
and miserable failure
he says
tapping his aluminum pen
on your forehead.

How else to explain
the receding
background noise
the sharpening
of microscopic
focus
tightening
your vision
to studied intensity?

And yes,
this is how it feels
gripping his throat
and *this*
is how
it feels
squeezing it.

October Knob and Broom

1.

Wind holds as the bonfires
grow crackle and spark
maple leaves fly away crows
caw and caw
what witness do you bear
jackdaw and superstition?

All Hallows' Eve
and my rusted hobgoblins
so many apples bobbing on icy waters
rise up shiver and haunt

Children bloated and sweet
grin like fat little pumpkins
of summer made flesh
predict gifts under a sharp and radiant moon

As I needle and crochet shawls
from my jagged bones
rattle cast and spin
tooth of the earth

and winter is a-coming soon

2.

(What do you fear?)

Postcard Written under a Halloween Flashlight from Camp Madness

Hi. Having an orangely tuneful time here. Today because I am a young beau-
tiful and said by private voices to be world's greatest poet, I was allowed to use
the Occ Ther Shop and I worked on a wall hanging I wove like the sky powder
blue steel loom and thread. Later, medication and the Imaginary Theater
Group came to visit the Happy Campers. And yes I am a Happy Camper here
at Camp Madness. I love my spin and fall, my secret that makes me special.
O Emily Dickinson, Sylvia P! Next time you come up please remember to
bring my postcard signed by the Pumpkin Queen that she will send to you
by dream tonight. On the front—To Laurel, Good Luck in the Future. Love,
Mary, Queen of Squash. On the back, this message—Stop Don't Stop Endit?
au secours au secours . . . Post Script. Even the owls can't be daunted, it's a starry
night on the campgrounds.

Sins

Hand-built sins
breadcrumb sins
small red grains
of memories lost
but not forgotten
the 1% crack
lack of preparation
flecks of character considered
monstrous in retrospect
my horrendous compendium
of guilt and retribution

This thing I know:
no blame was more
skillfully applied
poultice or corset
could not extract
subtract a venom
more lethal than my own
purchased on the common market
and at great expense

Come, rise up
stand clear-eyed
and shine amber
of truth
      whole truth
            silver-studded truth

Now my tongue holds a jewel
pearls its poison with flakes
of shell/breadcrumb sins
once monolith
dissolve like wafer in wine

Slow Questions Nudge Like a Gentle Intruder

I come here to set this down—
Outside the wind flaps
An old pair of drawers
My world howls for attention
A shower of gold visions
And inaudible praise

He stares at himself
Tufts and patches
I need to know
Which is real
Is love as real as a razor?
Will it blossom like a cut?
There is no time for blandness
When cocoons shudder to be opened

The moon rises flagrant
as a kept woman
I rouge my cheeks
To go out on the town.

SPANKINGS I'VE KNOWN

Silver steel brush
snarls and scrapes hair

you're a bad girl
Little Laurel Ann

go upstairs and get
your brush
is the pronouncement
and
     on the longest walk
                of my life

I fetch it

The Last Girl in the Land of the Butterflies

Abandoned by my life
I take flight
from the city of angels
in a cataclysm of vivid hues
cry and shriek of sirens
call me to lift my feet and eyes
from the ground

where once I wasted away
in the silent shadow of a stoplight
thin thin painful silhouette
hollow chest so shallow
I could not even breathe
sliver of self
disappearing in inky darkness

I fell and fell and fell asleep
until I could only fall
from the grace I never knew
in this lifetime
a tethered cocoon
muffled sobs leaking from midnight pipes
il purgatorio

and the clouds passed over the moon, yes

and then I opened my arms
and then I opened my eyes
and then I opened my heart

Now I stretch my webbed fingers
to the splintered sky and see wings of color
cross before me in the cobalt night

hold them close
hold them to me

The Mother's Room

and this too is me
the dull sheen of purple jersey
daughter as crone
and behind that door
the mother's room
unknown women tend her
blonde mother of the plains
silent girls offer reflections to kiss
a cord to my abdomen glistens and throbs

and she spins that cord
and she spins and she twists
and when she is old
she spins
and when she is dead
she spins

The Waldorf Astoria
(Family Album, New York, August, 1963)

Sitting at the Fairfax Theatre in Los Angeles
I thought of bellhops and Ginger Rogers.
Kiddie Matinee. I was, in fact, thirteen that summer
but looked younger: quiet, did what I was told
I liked the movies / lived in them

We had been the promised ones
two pet schnauzers / a leather harness to keep
my brother from straying
                                        me, a head taller,
reticent, rarely photographed

We wanted to be liked
I sniffed and curtsied
I'm a little teapot short and stout
he gallantly threw footballs and baseballs
in front of the white stucco house on Norton Avenue
while we waited for Davy Crockett to save us

But what we must have meant to my father
                                        "the family"
then, driving back to his boyhood home in upstate
New York / a transcontinental journey in a Cadillac
convertible with fins and a blonde shiksa wife
the baby brother who made good
the two of us, their offspring, the cousins from California
didn't know egg creams or the Automat
but were good kids (might have to smack 'em
around now and then)

I put *Mad Magazine* on the backseat floor
as we crossed the George Washington Bridge
slipped my shoes on and looked up at slab after slab
of buildings liked up in rows, blocking the sky
until I see flags and a man with gold epaulets on his uniform
standing outside a revolving doorway on Park Avenue
and Dad glides the Cadillac up to the curb,
runs his hands through his hair.

      Comes back out, says, "Helen,
we're staying at the Waldorf." Inside, my brother
slides across the polished marble floor of the lobby

like we belonged with the popular young president
who reigned in Camelot—

Nothing bad could ever happen to any of us.

Wings/That Which Takes Flight

—for Raymond Levin and H. Thomas Mauldin

We return to ourselves gradually
peel layers from squares
and squares of rice paper

I pick up a bamboo brush
dip it in ink
hold my breath
let it fly on the page
dip and stroke quickly
up again and across

Ravens against a barren field
in a January frost
shear the medieval sky
with their magnificent blackness
they arc and crest
cut the air deftly
above this walled city
leave a gash in their stead

I bind it with cloth and linen fiber
yet the ink spreads
across bodies and nations
I scuff my heels on the earthly rock
where I live, flung on an indigo canopy
this mechanism
chain and stone
paper, scissors, rock

this catapult
(paper, scissors, rock)

2000s

BORGIA, 2009

The names of the hungry
are written on prayer flags
that guard the crossroads—
all those sentinels holding off
an onslaught of need.

The hunger for money,
fame and power belongs
to the princes of ambition.
The hunger for knowledge,
carved over doors
of bulging libraries,
cannot be sated
by its ten million books.

My hunger is nameless—
a smiling ghost who mocks me
behind my portrait.
As for love, whether glutton
or starved, we can each
be poisoned.

Heliotrope

A cat, lounging
on the compost heap, nibbles
the bordering amaryllis.
Bulbs dream and seeds nod—
in Spring they'll bloom again.

Grief is not a shy bouquet
to hold close to your breast—
its petals want to foxtrot
and croon, and stems,
spangled like leggy chorus
girls, drip with garlands of jasmine.

Wherever the sun flowers, I lift
my face to the light and know everything
I've ever known and everything
I couldn't have guessed
would remember me.

Hollywood Hills Noir

—for Doug Knott

Aberration of weather studs
the sloe-eyed city where change
gels in ripples after due process
I could go deeper
pry open the locked vault
below, combustible fossils bubble
in tar and petroleum beneath
Wilshire Blvd.—the jacaranda's roots
divide the house
Los Angeles
erupts in violet blossoms
each spring the profusion
is uncontained by stucco

Nature needs tending, of course
every few years the plates shift
the photogenic councilman is arrested
and somebody takes a fall
That's how I came here—by a calling
as surely as the devil herself
cloaked in the need to be seen
in filtered light
latticed with fault lines
and an underground whirlpool
as profligate as oil.

I Dream the Light of Reason II

The Reasonable Woman is a hope chest, a locked cabinet.

The Reasonable Woman is pleasant enough.

The Reasonable Woman is the converse of sex.

The Reasonable Woman is a durable good, a sound diagnosis.

The Reasonable Woman is a subordinate clause.

The Reasonable Woman is childproof, although Heidi is already up to her knee.

The Reasonable Woman is a skillet, a war bond.

The Reasonable Woman is a fugue heard on the intercom.

The Reasonable Woman is a graph of stock options, the percentage of return.

The Reasonable Woman is open to suggestion.

The Reasonable Woman is a string bean, a cauliflower, a field of potatoes.

The Reasonable Woman is a packet of Alka-Seltzer in the Accounts Payable file.

The Reasonable Woman is considering bankruptcy.

The Reasonable Woman is a stacked heel, a running shoe.

The Reasonable Woman is a pair of pantyhose in the bathroom sink.

The Reasonable Woman is fat free.

The Reasonable Woman is a shadow of herself.

Why would The Reasonable Woman become unreasonable?

IMPRINT, MAY 1970

1.

I tell you the skin alone cannot contain
the brawl of a generation—
we burned flags before the helmets
and the dogs rabid with our parents' teeth.
Then we locked arms, swaying
and cheered when the match struck.
We watched, swore the jelly of napalm
would not silence the corpses
pulled from rice paddies in another world.

We thought our skin could still contain
the body blows, the clubs and guns
that struck down one
by one by one by one

2.

I shuffled through white china rows
of lunchtime professors
my black armband for the dead
the frat boys on scholarship
carrying thick-skinned pudding
trays of coffee and cream
counted the days until graduation
Mao and a map of Canada
hidden in their back pockets.

3.

A girl on the television in the foyer
bent down, transfixed, screaming
skin stretched taut to the corners
her arms outstretched, protesting
the body of the sprawled boy before her
blood seeps from sinew to dermis
her young face twists
when a camera clicks like a bullet
in a chamber of the heart and we are naive
as though fists had never bruised us before

I stopped dropped
the sheets of colored paper
like blood flowering
on the four-cornered floor.

4.

They say even Nixon broke
when they started killing the students
the rupture of skin splitting open
a wound even he could not stitch together
so when they told me it was over
I didn't believe them
that scar on membrane and flesh
smoothing over but will not slough off

My Celluloid Heroes

In whose dreams will these stars shimmer
100 light years from now?
Their blown-up images snipped
of imperfections—the errant mole,
an ingrown hair, when paste
does not pass for diamonds.

Confined by fame, Pilates and exfoliation,
tucked in canyons, behind gated walls,
some corner the market on chihuahuas
others collect bags of kudos.
They tell me Rodeo Drive is a state of mind.

As for mine,
                    it skims along
Hollywood Boulevard like a chauffeur.
From the back seat
I hear my voice
at home in the shadows—
I don't want to sleep yet, Bogen,
Drive.

I can see and not be seen—invisible to a world
in which I was born. Now you see
me, now you don't.

My Sentence

The noose of it
wears me big
I weigh and grind
the words with method
efficiency afraid
of what they might say
and punctuate of my life

At first I was confused
could not could not
could not not not
unknot the stray tangents
the first time I saw my mother
or the last kiss before sleep
wanted to round up order
and let meaning fall
where it may

Later I played it out
as it showed itself to me
coaxed my human mind
to mastery

I have served
my sentence with devotion
watched as it flailed
and rose on the page
becoming that which I could never be

poetry

Mystery Spot with Gaze Turned Inward

What vortex pulsates above my bed?
Sprawled among the flannel sheets
and four felines waiting to be fed,
he ponders these questions of ultimate
torque and consequence.
How the little wheels of his mechanism spin!
Great is his dynamo—a nuclear reactor
whirrs in his Kenmore guarantee.

I stick to him like gravity—
an inescapable pull
impels my Volkswagen
down the 2 to the 134
hurtling past freeway exits
taco stands and mini-marts
from Highland Park to Lake Street
past the tinted windows of Roscoe's House
of Chicken and Waffles,
the Planned Parenthood clinic whose clients
cup furtive joints in the parking lot,
the Craftsman house with the blue Christmas lights
where Lil' Kim blares from the porch.
Down the street, maple leaves pile
like dunes in his marvelous yard.
There, in the melting light, I stop
to measure the turbulence,
plant herbs, calibrate our inverse polarity,
wind socks flapping in the sun, an oscillation
of simple mysteries caught then funneled outward.

Poem

This is your last warning:
My orange lipstick smeared
on the stubbed out butt-
end of a Marlboro Lite
smoldering, in your favorite
booth at the last cappuccino
stand before the 405,

tells you I'm here:
the mean one.
Heinrich Himmler meets
Lizzie Borden.
And did I mention vengeful?
Just to remind you,
it was Craig Oulie
who pulled the arms off my Chatty
Cathy and sucked
the fingers like popsicles,
it was Felicia Lafferty
who eloped with my conflicted
boyfriend and it was you,
don't deny it, who devoured
the last of my Ben
and Jerry's Heath Bar Crunch
the single melting
spoonful an abandoned
mystery in the sink.

I'm the horrid one.
My face puce with apoplexy,
a loathsome toad you pretended
to kiss. I'm the Little Girl
with the curl right in the middle
of my forehead. So Go Ahead.

I'm the one you need
to sock in the eye.
Douse with gasoline.
Slice open with the shiv
of a madman.
Don't think about me.
Don't consider me.
Make me the one
you love to grind
beneath your boot-heel,
whose name leaves a bad
taste clotted
in your mouth like the turned milk
you spit out on broken pavement

Call me Nazi Girl,
Anti-Christ in a power suit.
I'm the one with the plastic
Beretta who taunts the SWAT team.
Kill Me.

The Door for Love and Death
—after Tomaz Salamun

You push the shadow against the wall.
Open the door for love and death.
What rooms are rented there?

In the room of Exquisite Torture,
A woman watches her lover shave.

In the Room of Hopeless Romantic,
A man weeps before a portrait of Voltaire.

In the Room of Maternal Instinct,
The rose is embalmed.

In the Room of Amorous Adventure,
Both doors hide the tiger.

In the Room of My Life,
I give up one and love the other.

The Quick Step

In the Celestial Ballroom
even the gnarled and ungainly,
the ones with fetid breath
folded in newspapers
or hands like gutted fish
will twirl their heels nimbly.
This time their arms won't flap,
and they won't collide with potted palms
or themselves. No man or woman

will hug the wall alone.
Yes, they will clap
Slow Slow Quick Quick Slow.
Their feet glide gracefully
where desired and they will be desired
by partners bowing in tuxedo and gown
while the bandleader sways again
to the Dance of the Wallflowers
in a room incandescent with stars.

Visibility Report

You cannot gaze into the divisions of a heart or the pulse that separates this world from the next, but I have seen the eyes of others drawn into themselves, a face pinched shut; in the half-light even need itself is obscured. Come closer—I am slate. Who will scratch their name on the empty stone with a penknife or erase its ridges from the template? The unopened gift is still a gift. It is given like a forecast or traffic report—background to common cash and carry or extraordinary good fortune. There's a high pressure front ahead: A hand is offered.

Take it.

Washing a Language

—*after Margaret Atwood, "Mute"*

Scrub the pitted roll-call
naming of parts
voiced in smoke and honey
or chattering wildly
never enough never enough

Bleach and soap and rinse
cold water to soak the stained
vowels—you cannot make crisp
linen from a polyester blend

Darling!
and I call myself that
throw out your microscope
the unrepentant bacteria are everywhere
an amoebaed city teems
in the dictionary of your brain
midnight laundry
                    what hope is there then
for absolution?
Fold, stack
(goddamn the rinse cycle's love
of those adulterous detergents)

Winchester Mystery House

Driving north to San Francisco
I'd see the signs:
"Winchester Mystery House—30 miles"
TraveLodge, Foster's Freeze, Burma Shave
"Winchester Mystery House—12 miles ahead."
Old Lady Winchester believed
that as long as the house remained
unfinished, she would live

and so built sliding floors, gilt-filled parlors
and staircases at the top of which a door
was slammed against heaven.
Yet, isn't that what we all want—
to stave off death with architecture
of our own design?
My intentions as twisted
as her polished oak banisters,
my blueprints muddy, walked over;
the windows open but do
not close, and above, a nucleated bulb
swings on its fraying cord.

I want to believe Old Lady Winchester,
I want to believe that if I hammer a yes
to another unknown closet,
lobe or unrequited need,
from what was fallow
will erupt a great mansion.

2010s

A Canticle for Bogen

Her body opens and closes its locks like the St. Lawrence Seaway.
Her eyes click click everything data whirring.
Her curls are antennae of grief.
Her ears hear the music of disappearing ink, and treasure maps
   torn from mattresses. Here there be dragons.
Her mouth mumbles stones in her mouth. Rivers of stones.
Her throat growls a secret language. She will not disclose its vocabulary.
Her voice wants its timbre to be heard.
Her shoulders hunch like hardened criminals.
Her breasts are outlawed in seven states.
Her lungs caress her furtive breath.
Her breath inhabits her lungs.
Her heart is big—when the wind blows from the south.
Her heart is a tent, oasis, magic lantern.
Her heart pulls aside the curtain and says Please Enter.
Her hands are tools to plant roses—fat floribunda and crimson blossoms
   unfurl despite themselves.
Her fingers are searchlights.
Her arms lifeboat your stormy SOS.
Her arms can carry you or your nightmare, you and your nightmare.
Ten thousand eggs sing in her ovaries.
Her girdled hips cry out revolution, sashay like Emma Goldman on Ecstasy.
Punch and Judy battle in her thighs.
Her toes are divining rods searching for gold.
She is the paradox of latency and hope.
She is the paradox of want and have.
Unleash her, she is your dog collar.
Sling her Great Chain of Being around your waist.
She wears your clothes when you sleep.
She sleeps in your dreams when you wake.

Death Valley 6.2

Who could stand
to live in such a place
where the only embrace you allow
is the desolate highway itself
a torn ribbon of ink
and the sound of that valley
what sound there is
is the endless whine
of your own tattered voice

These are the penned-in days
you stay alive just to taunt
the irony of its name
                    the breath
animating the tumbleweed
empties into the visible salvation
of post nuclear
light

In the arid moonscape
the husk that was once
your heart lies face up
on the valley floor.

Don't Ask/Don't Tell

Don't ask the jaw why it will not remember its breakage.

Don't ask the tissue not to bruise.

Don't ask if cringing will appease the ugly beast.

Don't ask the moon how to measure the square root of her tears.

Don't tell where you put the tears.

Don't tell where you hid the secret password.

Don't tell any word what just passed.

Don't tell the heart to stop beating—it might believe you.

Doppelganger Redux (Again)

She has haunted me for years—
my name pinned to her paper heart,
stuck with slivers of glass
and eyes milky with accusations.

She does not breathe
except to sigh *don't leave.*
But I cannot take her with me—
tethered and chained—
dragging her like a bad mood

This Lady With The Veil
says I will starve
to feed her
tear up tickets
to Invulnerable Street—
where the unreal city of ghosts
blurs its web.

Tomorrow she will make me god,
all she promises are miracles.
I will own what I thought
I could not own
when I'm unable to move
writing my way out of my life,
my illegible life.

Dreams You Will Never
Tell Anyone

The gills flash
and scale
ripples just
under the surface
an omen
of (no) money:
funds are slippery—
you will be unable to catch
the lucre as it eels
through your fingers

To dream
of scarabs
is to dream
of transformation
ore to liquid
liquid to vapor
best keep
this vision
close
to your breast
your night mind,
not your heart

When dreams
of lost keys
intrude
and the calliope
nudges tell no one
tell no one

tell no one
everything

Hairpieces
I've loved
men I've loved
hairpieces
on the men I've loved
never mention
the dreams
you have of them
to other men

In seismic
Los Angeles
you are all
latex and Emma Peel
kink of cortex
kicks clotted
bed sheets
to the bottom
of spinsterhood
you are inappropriate
you are inappropriate
you are inappropriate
is a mantra
never uttered
only dreamt

Happy & Why Not?

—after Mary Oliver

There is gratitude
for the firing of each synapse
that leaps mid-brain
when words enfold
the unbidden music
of the heart's percussion

How to breathe?
How to allow
the willing lungs to work on their own?

Then the motor skills—
the locomotion to dance—
               if need be—
or buckle under the weight of sorrow

In the sartorial blackness
of my youth
I made a profession
of my own despair.
My face radiated a fragility
that guttered in my voice
and I did not believe
in what I touched,
or kissed, or scorned.

But how, then, can I see
rambunctious streamers
where once were none—

each splendid with an insignia
of hope, of foolish courage
of—perhaps it is true—life.

Kisses I Remember

In 1969 Ray Olson kissed me in the front seat of his Rambler. He tasted like cigarettes and although I never smoked I still like that taste.

In 1958 I kissed my sister good-bye as she married her first husband. Four more were to follow.

In 1982 I went to a Tom Waits concert to avoid seeing KISS.

In 1976 Harley kissed me outside the Vagabond theater on Wilshire Blvd. When he ran his lips down my neck, my back arched and I spilled my purse all over the sidewalk.

In May 1995 Little Guy Bogen kissed my nose with his orange cat tongue. Sandpaper kiss.

In 1962 Robert Goulet kissed me on the forehead backstage at the Coconut Grove. I was 12.

Ray Levin, calling from Savannah, always says, "our kisses make us feel better." He should know.

In 1999 listening to Joni Mitchell reminded me that "in France they kiss on Main Street."

On December 7, 1971 my father leaned over me and kissed me while his tears splashed my face. It was the first time I realized that he liked me. The empty bottle of chloral hydrate mocked; the red light on the ambulance went around and around, the straps on the gurney held me like a sarcophagus.

In 1963 I kissed a mirror to see what I looked like in case James Bond came into my bedroom.

2009: John Harris, S. A. Griffin, Michael C Ford, and Sherman Pearl kissed me so they could be in this poem.

On July 14, 1992 I kissed my brother and wished him a Happy 40th Birthday. I watched as he unwrapped my gift: a baseball signed by Willie Mays, his hero.

The Kiss of the Spider Woman (1986)

In 1979 I kissed an envelope handwritten by Gene Wilder, *The World's Greatest Lover.*

In December 2004 I kissed Kathleen Lohr, Mark Beaver, Claudia Handler, Brad Dourif, Doug Knott, Janet Sager, Erica Erdman, Nichole Morgan, Jerry Garcia (not that one), Rick Dowlearn, Cindy Woods, Beth Ruscio, Becky Garcia, The Lively Ms. Lively, Linda Hoag, Michael Gall and Venesha Pravin before we listened to Dylan Thomas read *A Child's Christmas in Wales* on the CD player. Then we all drank too much champagne and orange juice and eggnog. I needed to go to sleep shortly thereafter.

In 1965 I kissed my grandmother's powdery face in the nursing home where she died six months later. She did not know me but I had been her favorite.

In 1998 I kissed Mark on the cheek. I swore to myself I would never let myself fall in love again. And I didn't.

Memo: A Thousand Sincere Apologies

We regret to inform
you that your life
           as you know it
has become irrelevant
and needs be terminated

Please remember to keep
your arms and legs
inside the compartment
uniformly pressed.
Do not look to the left
nor under your seats.
Yes, you may breathe.

We apologize
that we've lied
           to you.
We are not accountable
for the failings of others.
But we apologize for them too.

Midway

That's right kid I'm not trying to sell ya a bill o'goods
Love is still possible in this junky world
—Bob Flanagan

His eyes glitter like carnivals
the night clings to his hair
carelessly, sticky and thinning fast

take a chance he says
honky-tonk in his step
spend a buck
your fortune is secure
Juicy Fruit

other lovers kiss under neon
they have not yet learned to fear
daytime's wide angle
they put their faith in palms and rings
milk bottles

halfway through a guarded life
a calliope grinds
a tawdry tin tin tin
and I ride topsy-turvy
the gossip of possibilities
burns my ears

so much was in reach
but I missed the ring
                        blew the trick

I need my nets
my snake-eyed dice
that magic card
the fortune teller loaned me

Mon Père, The French Surrealist

(Or, This Is Not a Poem)

When the other French Surrealists come for dinner
my Father gives them Gauloises that explode
in random puffs. They had all complained
in their R.S.V.P. that life was boring.
I have a cure, he thought, and doctored
their aperitif with LSD to polish their vision
for the bifocaled world.

I ask my Father, Why the Surrealists?
Why not the Absurdists? Or the Existentialists
with their grand ennui? Why do they exist?
And what are they doing
in our sitting room?

Maurice practices his intensity, dart throwing
and competitive anxiety.
Pierre's specialty is self-observation
in a two-way mirror.
Cossette languishes sans romance.
Louis the Bulldog is also a parrot
grr grr squawk!
If you let him close
to your fingers, my father says
he will mistake them for fromage.
He loves fromage.

On the tote board of useful advice
my Father is king.

My Father's Hands

Caught fly balls,
forward passes as he dashed
across unshadowed fields,
flung the javelin to kingdom gone.

Later, splayed arthritic,
they seemed not to belong
to his body,
embarrassed him
with their need to hold.

Old man, did you not
think it would come to this?
Knobbed appendages unable
to grasp. Your back hunches
as the ripe fruit drops.

Seamstress of Disguise

She rummages through racks of costumes:
Sister Flossie of the Cross,
Russian Sonia, wolf hounds de rigueuer,
Bo-Peep Meets Little Red Riding Hood—
unable to choose which would be most gratifying
toe to toe with fear of flogging, fear of Bolsheviks,
fear of wolves with those pointy teeth?

Salome's veil would call hither
a murmuring crowd.
Or the standard Jeanne d'Arc variation
with circus hoop of fire
might inspire a more fervid response.

Ha-Ha! Notice me! Notice me!
Surely no one would suspect
her of this—Miss Mouse,
Miss Myopia, always handy
with thread.

O Audience, stitch your thimble-filled
conclusions into the orchestra pit.

Like a seam, she'll snip it.

Sweet Silver Pillbox
Mother of God

My etched lid belies
the coffin you choose:
    —Open me—
distorts the reflection of your face.

One pill, two pill.
Green pill, blue pill.
No mistake
I am the accident waiting for you to happen.

Taking Care of Futurism

Oh Futurism, I want to take
your pulse and listen
to your heartbeat
with an atomic stethoscope of love!
I'm tired of the past
with its ashcanned regret.
In the World of Tomorrow
you are New Year's Eve,
even if it's only November.
Your hi-def fingers tousle my hair.
Let's hijack the next open mind
that floats by on a sound waved air car,
hide under blankets with our socks on,
dine on dee vee dee dinners.
There are no eggplants of yesteryear
and today's only an hourglass
away from last week.
I don't want a goldfish or a ferret, only you.
I'll be your Clara Barton if you'll be
my Louis Pasteur. We can play
doctor all night, X-ray the interior
of the human heart. Find the darkness
behind what passes for history.
Now look what you've done—made me all poetic!
Dearest, you are the future of the future.

The Meeting of Tongues

Tongues whose lies sweeten lips like a sugar substitute.

Tongues with needles sew you to your crib.

Tongues of mayhem, tongues of deceit.

A probing tongue under a spotlight interrogates.

Tongues of lust, pink heart-warped desire.

Baby tongues, kitten tongues imprint: they know not what they know.

The tongue of authority lumbers in the square, stamps yes stamps no with polished boots.

Tongues of the city size you up, chew, swallow, or spit you out like a wad of pale gum.

The tongues of lawyers clack with herringbone lips.

Some tongues, strategically placed, will do maximum damage.

Some tongues are better left alone.

THE PLEASURES OF THE MIND

No apologies. I have enjoyed
contemplating, with much mental abandon,
the ruin of my enemies. *No apologies.*

Take, for example, the closure
of the shady antiquarian bookstore
whose owner, a short man
in the throes of a prolonged divorce,
had hired me, the only woman on staff,
to work out his gender issues.
Was I The Madonna or The Whore?
He could not decide whether to genuflect
or corner me in the stockroom.

What about those dreams as a child
where I would find myself
in nightly flight above a playground
filled with the nasty girls
who lived to torment me.
O Enola Gay I summon you
with your white heat and ash.

Then the heinous Bank of America,
the Anti-Christ I truly believe Incarnate:
Funder of the Vietnam War
a devil-dog that nearly hounded me to suicide
with overdraft
overdraft
those overdraft fees.
Going postal would have been too easy.

If only I had still been in possession
of my Good Little Nazi VW Beetle—
purchased on time on September 12, 2001—
and rammed it through the B of A's reinforced windows,
then I might have been thought a formidable woman.
But perhaps that cursed
automobile knew its true genesis
and, unloved, born of fear and obligation,
it rewarded me instead with a string of accidents
and citations.

To this day I relish the memory
of the pettiest of vandalisms I set loose
upon another vehicle whose driver,
a teenage girl slathered in makeup overkill,
stole my parking place
at the airport
on the night before Thanksgiving.
And then, seeing me fuming
behind my steering wheel, laughed.

I love how one learns so much from literature,
such as the chemical mixture and properties
of lanolin and lipstick,
or the way flying gravel pockmarks a windshield
as one kicks it up over asphalt.
The contents of the tube of Love That Red
I used to Revlon the word CUNT
on her windshield was bound
to hold its gaudy smear for weeks.

Things Tripped Over in the Dark

—for Chumley

First the box of my mother's photos,
squeezed in its passively aggressive corner.
Then magazines—
that cord to my former life—
all pulverized
and fed to the cat

Suddenly coughed up
like a hairball. O Horror!
It is too slick to stay swallowed,
greased with doubt, innuendo,
and Authority's Big Stick.

Against the credenza,
balled up
wads of fists
mewl
unsatisfied and unfed.

The detritus
of an over-examined life
strewn across a mirrored floor:
a packet of Saturday midnights
throws a dim silhouette of lovers
inexplicably bound,
long past caring
in mortal pas de deux.

Best not forget the slit
of a cat's eye opening,

all that ripples
between fur and skin,
a switchblade
of grass.

TILT

Some god is white gloved nervous
punch drunk and squeezes his fist
back to the planetary wall
head buzzing with static

some god wants to hit something—
any thing will do
                    make a big noise
plates that screech and grunt
                    wants to push
up against it
an Edward G. Robinson tough guy
no machine can contain

snap goes the fuse
some god detonates the garden party
umbrellas and lily pads flutter at noon

Notes

Defectives

Adolphe Menjou (1890-1963): dapper American character actor who epitomized the "man about town" persona

juliettes: a type of manicure

I Coulda Been a Contender

Gordon Lightfoot: Canadian folk singer popular in the 1960s and '70s

Ali shuffle: reference to the fancy footwork of heavyweight boxer Muhammad Ali

---

Mary Magdalene Crosses the Delaware

English Leather: an inexpensive men's cologne with a lingering scent

---

Narrow Beds

Southern Comfort: an American liqueur made from neutral spirits with fruit, spice, and whiskey flavoring. Because of its sweetness, the strength of its alcoholic proof was often disguised.

Three Years Later I Still Send Anonymous Postcards To You

Roy Rogers on Trigger: a TV cowboy and his horse popular in the 1950s

---

Detective Supremo

Mickey Finn: a knock-out drug, often spiked in drinks of an unsuspecting victim

Detective Supremo Meets Her Match

Nick Charles: AKA The Thin Man. Urbane private detective who, along with his wife Nora, solved various crimes in books and films of the 1930s and '40s.

I Eat Lunch with a Schizophrenic

Timex: an inexpensive brand of watch.

Pigmy Headhunters and Killer Apes, My Lover and Me

Vidal Sassoon: British hairdresser who later founded an international brand of hair treatments and products.

Musso and Frank: an "old Hollywood" restaurant, founded in 1919. It is said that the ghost of F. Scott Fitzgerald walks there.

Mom and the Goldfish

Rod McKuen: a best-selling American poet in the 1960s, who was never taken seriously by literary critics.

Love of Shoe

Native Dancer: famous thoroughbred horse.

The Möbius Strip

Cyd Charisse: dancer often featured in film musicals with Fred Astaire and Gene Kelly.

"gotta dance": phrase called out by Gene Kelly in the 1952 musical *Singin' in the Rain*.

FISSION

Eli Lilly: pharmaceutical company.
WASP: White Anglo-Saxon Protestant.

HOMESTEAD

victory garden: also called war gardens or food gardens for defense; vegetable, fruit, and herb gardens planted at private residences and public parks in the United States, UK, Canada, and Germany during World War I and World War II. They were used to reduce pressure on the public food supply and raise morale.

MORNING FEVER 11 A.M.

Appointment in Samarra: The following is a retelling of an old folk tale, later made famous by W. Somerset Maugham. A merchant in Baghdad sends his servant to the marketplace for provisions. Shortly, the servant comes home white and trembling and tells him that in the marketplace he was jostled by a woman, whom he recognized as Death, and she made a threatening gesture. Borrowing the merchant's horse, he flees at top speed to Samarra, a distance of about seventy-five miles where he believes Death will not find him. The merchant then goes to the marketplace and finds Death, and asks why she made the threatening gesture. She replies, "That was not a threatening gesture, it was only a start of surprise. I was astonished to see him in Baghdad, for I had an appointment with him tonight in Samarra."

POSTCARD WRITTEN UNDER A HALLOWEEN FLASHLIGHT FROM CAMP MADNESS

Sylvia P: Sylvia Plath.
Mary Queen of Squash: play on words "Mary, Queen of Scots."
au secours: French word meaning *help*.

The Waldorf Astoria (Family Album, New York, August, 1963)

kiddie matinee: promotion used by many movie theaters in Los Angeles in the late 1950s and '60s to show films geared for children during the summer and/or on Saturdays to get them out of their parents' hair for a few hours.

Mad Magazine: popular satirical magazine originally published as a comic book; later influenced generations of disenfranchised young people.

egg creams: chocolate fizzy drink (has no eggs in it).

Automat: a fast-food cafeteria restaurant where all food and drink are served by coin- and bill-operated vending machines.

My Celluloid Heroes

Title is in reference to the song *Celluloid Heroes* by British rock band The Kinks (circa 1972).

Paste: fake or costume jewelry was often called *paste*.

Winchester Mystery House

Travelodge: motel chain.

Foster's Freeze: a chain of ice cream stands.

Burma-Shave: brand of brushless shaving cream famous for its advertising gimmick of posting humorous rhyming poems on small sequential highway roadside signs.

Dreams You Will Never Tell Anyone

Emma Peel: name of character played by Diana Rigg in the British television show *The Avengers*.

Afterword

I come here to set this down . . . so begins my poem "Slow Questions Nudge Like a Gentle Intruder" and so this begins as well.

How to separate the art from the artist? My art, my words, I've hoped would speak for me, no explanations necessary. Beyond that, I have attempted to create poems that are idiosyncratic yet have a universal, albeit often intense, baseline. Are they the truth? The emotional truth? Or the literal truth? If I wrote about the day my grandmother died, would it matter if Narrator Laurel wore a blue blouse when in the real world Historical Laurel wore an orange plaid one?

The more time I spent looking back and choosing poems for this collection the more I realized that I had been given a gift: the opportunity to look at my life's work—my poetry—and judge its worthiness in my own eyes.

I often tell students that every creative act requires a critical one, the ability to step backwards and say "this pleases me" or "this doesn't work." Because it is only through our dissatisfactions with what we have created that we are given the impetus to go forward and finish what we have started.

No one writes in a vacuum. I am very grateful to the editors and early champions of my work, especially Kathleen Bregand, Peter Schneidre, Bill Mohr, Ron Koertge, Steve Kowit, Michael C. Ford, Wanda Coleman, Charles Harper Webb, Holly Prado, Harry Northup, Elliot Fried, Rosa Cumare, Suzanne Lummis, Raymond Levin, H. Thomas Mauldin, and Clayton Eshelman. Without their encouragement, I doubt that I would have continued.

Other friends and family provided invaluable support upon what can only be called a perilous undertaking: Doug Knott, Beverly Hay, Kathleen Lohr, Robin Conerly, Linda Fry, Linda Albertano, D. Frank Culbertson, Raymond Constantine, Sherry Modell, Janet Klein, Ann Cavanaugh, Sandra Roggero, Mark Poyser, Dani Roter, Alan and Andrea Rademan, the Bogen and Ramsay clans, the Right Honorable Sir Chumley of Amherst, and the many students whose friendship has enriched my life.

Biographical Note

Laurel Ann Bogen is a poet, teacher and performance artist who embodies the concept of a thirty-year overnight sensation. The author of ten books including *Washing a Language* and *The Last Girl in the Land of the Butterflies*, Bogen has taught in the UCLA Writer's Extension Program since 1990 and is also a founding member of the celebrated poetry performance ensemble, Nearly Fatal Women. She lives in Los Angeles.